£4

THRUMS AND THE BARRIE COUNTRY

THE BARRIE COUNTRY

THRUMS AND THE BARRIE COUNTRY

BY

JOHN KENNEDY, B.D.

ILLUSTRATED

HEATH CRANTON LIMITED
6 FLEET LANE   LONDON E.C.4
1930

Printed in Great Britain for Heath Cranton Limited by
Northumberland Press Limited, Newcastle-on-Tyne

PREFACE

THIS book evolved out of a close acquaintance
with the Barrie country in a three years'
ministry spent in the town of Forfar. The
country has a charm of its own, as has also Barrie.
I have endeavoured to trace Barrie's connection
with its soil—to show something of the history
of Kirriemuir, to reveal the heritage and early
environment of the greatest of her sons, and to
provide a guide to the streets and glens made
famous in his stories.

It is often said that Kirriemuir is not proud
of Barrie—that it is dead to his greatness and
indifferent to his fame. That is only partly true.
Kirriemuir does not boast of Barrie, but then it
does not boast of anything. It is not in the
Scottish nature to reveal the secrets of the heart.
Whether Kirriemuir is proud of Barrie or not the
stranger shall never know. His nimble wit has
played over the little red town like summer
sunshine, and, like the sunshine, it has been
accepted without remark.

As Barrie himself says, the outsider cannot
understand the Scot's mentality. The Sassenach

5

thinks him dull and heavy, wanting in vivacity and expression. That may be so. But it is only a surface impression. To understand the Scot one must understand him in his home. There in the love of " wife and weans," the neighbourly self-sacrifice in days of hardship, the devotion to the dear glen and the eternal hills the Scot is revealed at his best. It does not make for communicativeness, for the good Scot does not speak of the deep matters of his soul, but it makes for depth and power. " Still waters run deep." It is so in Kirriemuir and Angus.

It is because of this that the Kirriemarian himself does not understand Barrie. He does not see why he should write about the things that lie so dear to his heart. That he should reveal the secrets of the family to the world, that he should make literature out of " old forgotten things," is to him a thing inexplicable. In this sense Barrie himself is not a true Kirriemarian. A real son of the toonie on the hill would have " kept these things and pondered them in his heart."

Barrie had to go to England to learn the art of self-expression. He had to stand afar off and see things through a glass darkly, and let his rosy fancy play on them before a little cottage on a brae loomed through the haze to be peopled with creatures of his fancy. It was when he saw Kirriemuir from a distance and through English eyes that he realized that it was quaint, that the home-life there was sweet above all else, and its glens were bonny compared to English meadows.

6

In that, at least, he was a true son of Kirriemuir, for every man of that little town loves his native place.

But go to Kirriemuir to-day and inquire of Barrie and few will seek to tell his story. They do not resent his communicativeness now, though once upon a time they did. They simply do not understand it. So no one has attempted to follow him up and proclaim *his* story to the world. That this book sets out to do as far as concerns Kirriemuir and district. It is a story worth the telling. The rise of a weaver's son to be the doyen of English literature is no mean feat. To those who have made the story easy of the telling, I tender grateful thanks. Mr. John F. Mills of Kirriemuir and Mr. R. W. Dill of Forfar were foremost in kindness among the men of the North, while the helpful suggestions of my friends, Mr. John M. Jack and Mr. J. G. Fyfe, have only deepened a debt of gratitude which was always great.

JOHN KENNEDY.

THE MANSE,
    OLD KILPATRICK.

NOTE.—I am indebted to Messrs. Valentine of Dundee for permission to reproduce the photograph of the Auld Licht Kirk, and to Mr. John Grant for permission to reproduce the photograph of the Cottage on the Brae. I have also to thank Mr. John S. Whyte of Forfar for the use of his photograph of the School Group in Forfar.

THRUMS AND THE BARRIE COUNTRY

Messrs. Hodder & Stoughton, Ltd., and Messrs. Cassell & Co. Ltd. have allowed me to make extracts from Barrie's works, which kindness I gratefully acknowledge.

J. K.

CONTENTS

LIST OF ILLUSTRATIONS

PLANS

THE PAGEANT OF TIME

THE PAGEANT OF TIME

THE little red town of Kirriemuir nestles among the foothills of the Grampians in the historic county of Angus, five miles north-west of the county town of Forfar. It is not at all prepossessing to the eye, with its low-roofed " buts and bens " and crooked wynds. Barrie himself suggests that it is " gey an' mean an' bleak," so we must not say that it is otherwise. But like some old dame of ancient lineage, she can afford to dress in shabby clothes if it pleases her mind to do so. She is so rich in tradition and famous sons that she can be neglectful of appearances. Those who truly know her are not deceived, and she herself rather enjoys the disappointment of the stranger.

Kirriemuir is rich in her children. It was out of her borders there came the famous Sir Charles Lyell, who by his story of the rocks helped forward the thesis of the epoch-making Darwin. He was buried in Westminster Abbey with all due honours as the greatest geologist of his day. From the same little township there came the famous Alexander Whyte, a humble working woman's son, who rose to be minister of " Free St. George's," Edinburgh. And then, as if to prove conclusively that her mean exterior was no indication of poverty of soul, from the same class of working folk she sent J. M. Barrie to reveal her to the world.

She may not have asked for that revelation, but it would have been a pity had it not been given.

Her own interior greatness is not the richest thing about her. The district where she has made her home is rich in natural beauty. If Kirriemuir is bleak, her surroundings are magnificent; behind her the mighty Grampians stretch in majesty to the sky, before her feet sleeps the valley of Strathmore, with hamlets and forests and silver lochs making as fair a prospect as will be seen in Scotland. And on the southern side of the valley lie the gentle Sidlaws fading towards the sea. No smoke but the smoke of Forfar disturbs the scene, except the wreath of steam from a passing engine dragging its freight round the Grampians to the north.

She is rich in history and tradition. Battles have been fought there in the days of long ago. The battle-cry of the Romans has subdued the clamour of the Picts. Missionaries have come in peaceful embassy singing their songs of faith. And in the days of romantic story, men have ridden forth to fight for Charles Edward. While crowning all in simple pathos stands a cemetery on a hill where Margaret Ogilvy and David Barrie sleep, two types of humble weaver folk whose story their son has told. The roar of the power mills in the town, and the crying of the curlew in the fields may now drown the voices which would speak to us from the past, but to him who has ears to hear they still can speak and tell a story that is not ignoble.

If we would understand the story of Angus we must start with the coming of the Romans. About the year A.D. 80, Agricola came to Scotland

and forced his way northwards right to the foot of the Grampians. He left a camp at Kirkbuddo, some ten miles from the mouth of the Tay, and pushed a road straight northwards to within three miles of the present Kirriemuir. There, at a place called Battledykes, he laid down another camp and, with means of communication established between Battledykes and the sea, sought to hold the country against the onslaughts of the Picts.

The Picts from the fastnesses of the Grampians looked down on the Roman invader. Hitherto they had been defeated because of their want of leadership. They had been driven from the marshes and the plains and hemmed back in the inhospitable mountains, but there they rallied themselves and swore to be revenged. Their leader was Calgacus, a brave chieftain who for once was able to assume supreme command, and under his inspiration they gathered themselves in the highland glens, and prepared for a desperate throw with their all-conquering enemy. Blessed by the attendant Druid priests, they streamed down wildly to the plain. The Romans met them in steadfast order. The impulsive Picts made the first advance.

> " *Spearman and charioteer and bowman*
> *Charged and were scattered into spray.*
> *Savage and taciturn, the Roman*
> *Hewed upwards in the Roman way.*"

It was useless. The wild onslaught of the Picts was of no avail against the discipline of the Romans.

" There—in the twilight—where the cattle
Are lowing home across the fields,
The beaten warriors left the battle
Dead on the clansmen's wicker shields."

The battle of Mons Graupius was fought and lost.

But the Romans came no farther. They never penetrated the Grampians. Their roads run straightly beneath their mighty shadows questing for a passage-way, but that passage never was found. In Caddam Wood, where the Little Minister first saw Babbie dancing in the moonlight, and over the hill from Battledykes to Forfar, you will find traces of their passing, but mouldering leaves and earth have covered up the scene of combat.

When the Romans had passed and gone there came another invasion; but an invasion not to the blaring of the bugles but to the singing of psalms. Christian missionaries came in their mild embassy from England, carrying the Gospel into these wild Northern lands. Not but what Christian missionaries had been there before. Shortly after he landed at Iona, St. Columba and two companions had penetrated Pictland by the line of what is now the Caledonian Canal. They had met Brude, the Pictish king, not far from Inverness, and he and his people had been baptized. We may surmise that their influence had extended to the southward portion of Brude's territory, but it could never have been very strong. At any rate, in the seventh century A.D. the influence of Celtic Christianity in Pictland was waning. There were deeper influences penetrating from the South.

18

The monks of Northumbria were sending their embassies northwards, and at last in the year A.D. 710, at the express invitation of Nectan, the Pictish king, they came as far as Angus. Nectan met the embassy at a little place called Restenneth, one mile east of the present county town of Forfar, and there at the hands of St. Boniface (or Curitan, as he was otherwise called) he and his people were baptized. A little wooden chapel with a big square stone tower was founded at the side of the old Roman road which had led the monks into the kingdom, and on the edge of Restenneth Loch, where they fished for supper on Fridays, the monks raised their voices in praise amid the darkness of a heathen land. The old square tower still stands, and is one of the oldest ecclesiastical structures in Scotland. The kingdom, heathen in its ways, but nominally Christian in its faith, was given over to the care of St. Peter, and Pictland had Peter as its patron saint until the rise of the cult of St. Andrew.

The scene now changes to the coming of Queen Margaret. To the lover of Barrie this episode in the history of Angus has a more than passing interest. For the house in which he lived as a boy in Forfar is just under the shadow of Castle Hill, where the castle of Malcolm Canmore stood in olden days. Here to his stronghold in 1069 or thereabouts Malcolm brought his bride. She was beautiful, we are told, and learned, with a passion for reformation. The monks at Restenneth nearby must have resented her coming, for she bade them peremptorily to change their ways. Worship, which was after the Culdee style, was reformed to the Roman model, alms were most

19

the battle of Sheriffmuir. There, in fighting for him, he was slain. At nightfall Argyle, the leader of the opposing army, was riding over the field, when he saw a richly attired body lying on the ground with a retainer bending over it. " Wha's that man there? " Argyle asked gruffly, pointing to the body. " He was a man yesterday," came the grim reply from the trusty and broken-hearted guardian of the Lord of Strathmore.

In the " forty-five " the local family that suffered most for the cause was the house of Airlie. Lord Airlie, when Charles raised his standard, gathered full six hundred men around him from the glens of Cortachy and the wynds of Kirriemuir. They rode off to Edinburgh in high spirit, and followed their Prince through all his varied fortunes as he marched through England and back from England to Culloden. From that fatal field young Airlie never returned, but his sword was brought back to Cortachy Castle where it remains, a precious possession. It has inscribed on its hilt the legend, " The man who feels no delight in a gallant steed, a bright sword, and a fair ladye, has not in his breast the heart of a soldier."

It was in such a country that Barrie was born, a countryside of beauty and romance and " battles long ago." But although it provides a worthy background for his genius, he did not find his inspiration there. Sometimes an echo from the past steals through his books, as in the Jacobite Rebellion in *Sentimental Tommy*, but it was bent-backed weavers toiling at their looms, and arguing about the destiny of Church and State that provided him with material for his pen. He dealt with the environment with which he was most familiar, where the people were not ghosts but men of flesh and blood. We have now to take up the story of more modern days, not too modern, for the Auld Licht weavers if they came alive to-day would be strangely ill at ease. They were, however, sufficiently near Barrie to let him hear the accents of their tongues. It was not hard for him to penetrate their secrets who had Margaret Ogilvy for his mother, and genius as his lucky star.

THRUMS—WITH THE AULD LICHT MANSE IN FOREGROUND

THE HANDLOOM WEAVERS

THE Kirriemuir that Barrie writes about dates from the days of the " forty-five " and goes on to the time of the coming of machinery. He called it Thrums. The first question we ask ourselves is, Why did he call it that?

Thrums is a technical term used in weaving. It means the fringe of threads left on a loom when the web is taken off. These threads are spare, and a bunch of them will hang at the weaver's side when next he weaves a web. If a thread breaks on the loom, he will take a thrum and tie the two loose ends together. Barrie was a weaver too, tying loose ends of incident and character together.

Thrums also described the period of which he was writing. If you go to Kirriemuir to-day you may not see a thrum. They are there, but they are hidden from the stranger's eye in two great factories. In the handloom-weaving days, however, thrums were conspicuous everywhere. A weaver would tie up his breeches at the knee with a bunch of thrums, he would repair the deficiency of his " gallaces " with thrums, he would make a fancy watch-chain out of thrums, he would tie up his parcels with thrums, but the reign of thrums was over when the handloom days ended. With the coming of machinery thrums were buried in the factories and seen no more.

The Thrums community included, of course, more than the handloom weavers. It was composed of weavers, spinners, government inspectors, crofters, farmers, shopkeepers, tradesmen, and made up, indeed, a fair-sized town. The population in 1755 was 3,409, and in 1811, when handloom weaving was about its height, 4,791. In 1921 the population had dropped to 3,135, so that the Thrums that Barrie wrote about was bigger than the Kirriemuir of to-day. We cannot think of it as a struggling hamlet or even as a fair-sized village. It was a town, and possessed a Parish Church, an Episcopal Church, and two dissenting Churches, not to speak of the Auld Licht Kirk. But Barrie selected his material and so closely did he keep to his original choice, that one sometimes gets the impression that Thrums was peopled by a handful of Auld Licht weavers only.

Of the religious life of the community, we shall write in the next chapter. Sufficient to say here that Barrie again selected and wrote of the religious life he knew. He himself was brought up in a Free Church home and knew little of Auld Kirk folk and Episcopalians. Between the Churches then there was a great gulf fixed, as great as the gulf to-day between the average Protestant and the average Roman Catholic.

Thrums means for the reader of Barrie's books the Kirriemuir he knew. To put it more precisely, it means the old-time Kirriemuir known to Margaret Ogilvy and looked at through her eyes, for Barrie, as we shall come to see, drew most of his reminiscences from her. It is the Kirriemuir known to a working-class woman, who had a genius for a son.

The folk that Margaret Ogilvy knew were the spinners and the weavers. Both did their work at home, the spinning particularly being done by womenfolk. Every crofter's cottage in those days had its spinning-wheel to eke out the produce from the land. When the work of the day was over the gude-wife would sit by the fireside and there, by the light of the " cruizey," would spin the yarn for her gude-man to take to the weekly market. Many were the crofts which supported a large family on the joint labour of the husband and his helpmate. It is not the deer forest that has ousted the crofter from the land, it is the coming of the giant steam. When steam spinning mills began, spinning by hand went under, a consideration which might save us all from spurious oratory and from fruitless tears.

The weaver also worked at home, assisted by his wife and family. Sometimes " ben the hoose " there would be as many as four handlooms with a father and his sons or daughters manipulating the treadles and sending the shuttles flying to and fro. These were the days of large families, for every child was a wage-earner as soon as he could work. They were the days, too, of interminable noise. There was not much peace in a row of houses when two or three weavers in every back room were working from six in the morning till the gloaming, or longer if they so desired. They were the days, too, of exhausting labour. A weaver was bent and old before his time. The first noticeable sign of the improvement steam had brought, we are told by Barrie, was that one could walk through Kirriemuir and see straight-backed men and women.

The wages were very low, compared with wages nowadays. The average daily wage of a weaver even in the best times was one and fourpence. That of a spinner was a shilling. We are told of one authentic case where a weaver for a wager wove a web of 91 yards in eighteen hours. We may be sure he was a good craftsman or he would not have set himself out to create a record. Yet the price he received was eight shillings. Before machinery was introduced, the average weekly wage of a weaver was twelve to fourteen shillings. The children in the house might make five or six or seven. Nevertheless on these wages men brought up large families and even sent their sons to college.

Of course, in those days the purchasing value of money was greater, but only for the necessities of life. Many things that we count necessities were regarded as highest luxuries. At the end of the eighteenth century, only two tea-kettles were used in the whole of Kirriemuir, and that in a town of over four thousand souls. At the beginning of the nineteenth century, as late as the battle of Waterloo, the taste of China tea to many of the housewives was a thing unknown.

The houses the weavers lived in were composed in the main of a " but " and " ben," the " but " being the kitchen and the " ben " being the loom-shop. Perhaps off the kitchen there would be a little bedroom. Maybe, as in Aaron Latta's house in *Sentimental Tommy*, there would be a low-roofed attic reached from the kitchen by a ladder. No carpets were on the floor, sometimes not even boarding—earth trodden hard was all the protection afforded against cold and damp. This was not the mark of destitution. It was just the usual thing. The kitchen was the living-room, bedroom, dining-room and drawing-room. The " best room," beloved of Victorian housewives, used for the reception of the minister and for family parties, had not yet been invented. Indeed, when it did come, in many cases it was only the old loom-shop glorified. It was one of the " blessings " brought by steam.

Besides the work which was done in houses much work went on in loom-shops, where as many as ten to twenty looms were gathered together owned by a manufacturer. It is quite possible that Barrie's father was, for a time at least, in charge of one of these loom-shops, for we are told in *The Life of Alexander Whyte* by Dr. Barbour that " it was no ordinary treat for Alec Whyte when Mr. Barrie had a consignment of cloth to dispatch, to wriggle in among the webs, and so find a snug resting-place in the cart as it jolted on its way towards the city " (Dundee).

The significance of the loom-shop was that it prepared the way for the modern factory. The coming of steam only completed a process of centralization which had already begun.

The weaver had well-defined characteristics which have been sketched by a faithful hand in the Barrie books. He was independent, argumentative, thrifty, with a keen desire for knowledge. He was all that, of course, because he was a Scot, but something is also due to the conditions of his labour.

Each man, with few exceptions, was his own master. He owned the loom " ben the hoose " and was responsible for his own output. This fostered an independence which has not always maintained itself since the coming of machinery, and it was this independence which fostered the characteristics we have noted. He called no man his master. It is true that he was " sair hodden doon " by the restrictions of the Government, and many a time he was at the mercy of the manufacturer for the purchase of his web, but he did his work in his own time and in his own way, and called his soul his own.

His independence fostered his argumentativeness, and he would argue with any man at any time on any question. He thought deeply, if narrowly, on questions affecting both Church and State. The following incident, related by a minister, of handloom weaving days over fifty years ago is typical of many. At the beginning of his ministry he called on a handloom weaver on his pastoral visitation. " I'm real glad to see you, minister," the old man said, " for I'm sair needin' your help. I've been debatin' in my mind a' day what was the precise point o' the freedom o' the will that was affected by the Fall." Take away the theological setting of that question, archaic now but fresh and fertile then; alter it to a simple query such as this, " How far is man free? " and you will see something of the philosophic temper of the old-time weaver.

This thirst for knowledge was hardly met in the scant literature of the day. Books were few. The first book-shop in Kirriemuir was opened just before Barrie was born. The only literature that came into the place before that time came by the carrier's cart. Once a week he would bring *Chambers's Journal* and *Cassell's Educator* or maybe, *rara avis*, for the doctor, a copy of *Punch*. How eagerly they were read! The weavers stood in groups till the carter came, plucked them from

him as eagerly as we pluck our " latest special," and
hurried home to devour them by the flickering
" cruizey." They were passed from hand to hand,
one copy serving a dozen readers, till their frayed
and tattered pages would stand the strain no more.
Barrie has described it all, as it happened in more
exclusive circles, in *Sentimental Tommy*.

The travelling packman brought the books.
The *Pilgrim's Progress*, *Paradise Lost*, Dante's
Comedy, Whiston's *Josephus* and, of course, the
Bible, all came to be precious possessions valued
according to the discipline and the thrift that had
gone to win them. No wonder the big " Ha'
Bible " became a family heirloom. It would have
required a fortnight's weaving to get another.

But the dominating interest of the handloom
weaver, before the introduction of machinery, was
" The Charter." This stormy petrel of political
life is now so far forgotten that a summary of its
contents may be of value. It was drafted by
Francis Place, after the disappointing results of
the Reform Bill of 1832, and its main provisions
were as follows : Universal Suffrage, the Ballot,
Annual Parliaments, Payment of Members, Equal
Electoral Districts, and Abolition of Property
Qualifications. Barrie's father was a Chartist, as
indeed most of the weavers were. It gave rise to
the greatest upheaval known in the history of
Kirriemuir.

This " riot," as it was called, provided so much
material for Barrie in his novel *The Little Minister*
that an account of it is necessary. It occurred in
1839, just after the depression resulting from the
Napoleonic wars had become acute. The manu-
facturers of the day felt they must reduce the prices

THE AULD LICHTS

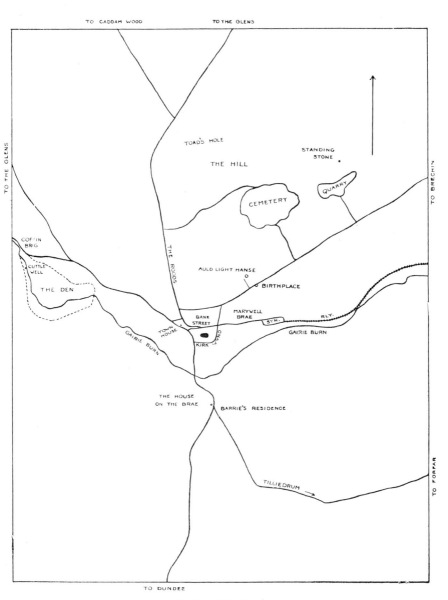

TO CADDAM WOOD   TO THE GLENS

TO THE GLENS

TO BRECHIN

TOAD'S HOLE

THE HILL

STANDING STONE

CEMETERY

QUARRY

COFFIN BRIG

THE ROODS

AULD LIGHT MANSE

BIRTHPLACE

CUTTLE WELL

THE DEN

GAIRIE BURN

TOWN HOUSE

BANK STREET

MARYWELL BRAE

STN.

RLY.

GAIRIE BURN

KIRK YARD

THE HOUSE ON THE BRAE

BARRIE'S RESIDENCE

TO FORFAR

TILLIEDRUM

TO DUNDEE

GUIDE to THRUMS

THE AULD LICHTS

TO the religious prejudices of the handloom weavers we must devote a chapter, always remembering that the weavers Barrie writes about did not represent the whole community. Indeed, in Kirriemuir to-day nothing is more noticable as one walks through the streets than the remnants of old religious differences which still hang about its walls. North from the square is the Roods, bringing to mind the Roman Catholic days when the principal street was the highway along which, on Saint's days, was carried by the monks the Cross of our Saviour. Not far from it is Elder's Close, suggesting a different ecclesiastical dominion, when the priestly hierarchy were swept away and session and presbytery were guardians of the morals of the people. Farther on we find Seceders' Close, speaking of a time when Presbyterianism was at war within itself and dissenting chapels were being hastily reared beside the Auld Kirk. It is interesting to notice that they are all narrow and crooked, reflecting, perhaps, the theological tenets of those who built them for their use. But they all lead into one another. That is a hopeful sign.

It is with Seceders' Close that we are principally concerned, for it was of the men who built it that Barrie wrote. Still we must not ignore the rest. All through the seceding days there were Moderates and Episcopalians occupying a far greater part in the life of Kirriemuir than Auld Licht stalwarts ever did. The Episcopalians had gone on their quiet and self-sacrificing way ever since Stewart days. The Moderates had held their own with dignity and with no small amount of social service. The Auld Lichts obeyed their conscience, and there was good and bad in the outlook of all of them.

Barrie wrote of the Auld Lichts because he knew them, and because, as we have suggested, he knew only them. In the intense religious feeling of the times the Jews had no dealings with the Samaritans. He was probably never inside the Auld Established Kirk, still less that of the Episcopalians. And, if the truth be spoken, it is highly probable he was never inside the Auld Licht Kirk itself, though he wrote so much about it. His people were not Auld Licht. They belonged to the South Free Church which disjoined itself from the Established in 1843. He left Kirriemuir when ten years old, and we may be sure that until that time he was kept rigidly by his parents to his own denomination. We can hardly fancy a boy of that tender age wandering off to other Churches in a thirst for wider knowledge, or even for a kind of melancholy pleasure. Barrie, we say, knew the South Free Church and no other during his time in Kirriemuir.

For the benefit of the uninitiated we give a short history of the Auld Licht Kirk and its relation to other Churches. It began in 1733 when Ebenezer Erskine and three other ministers of independent mind broke away from the Establishment on the question of the right of a congregation to nominate its own minister. (An act had just been passed, in 1732, placing that right in the hands of "the majority of the elders and heritors, if Protestants.") They were soon joined by others, and in a few years' time Secession Churches were springing up from end to end of the country.

This new Church was not without its difficulties. One of the most prominent was the relation between Church and State. This was settled in the Established Church by the text of the National Covenants, which gave the State power to interfere in Church affairs. A party in the new Church were for an interpretation of the Covenants which would more or less repudiate that power. They were known as the New Lights. Another party adhered to a literal interpretation of the Covenants, even though it included subjection to the State. They were known as the Old Lights. Their position was illogical, but it represented no trifling with fundamentals. And that was the keynote of the Auld Lichts through and through. It was they who possessed the Auld Licht Kirk written about by Barrie.

The Church which Barrie himself attended was of very much later origin and demands to modern readers little explanation. It arose at the Disruption in 1843. At that time the Church of Scotland was split in twain over the never-settled questions of patronage and the relation 'twixt Church and State. Along with half his brethren, the Rev. Daniel Cormick of South Parish Church in Kirriemuir left the shelter of the Establishment and formed the South Free Church. Among those who came out with him were Barrie's parents, and in a low-roofed building in the Glamis Road, young James Barrie, twenty years after, received his religious education.

At that time there was no connection between the Auld Lichts and the Frees, but in Barrie's own family there *was* a connection of which, in later days, he was to take full advantage in his Auld Licht stories. His mother, Margaret Ogilvy, had been brought up in the Auld Licht Kirk before her marriage to David Barrie. Her father, a stone mason, was a staunch Auld Licht supporter, and as her mother died when she was eight years old, she was his constant companion at its services. It was she, with her wealth of reminiscences, who supplied her son with the material for his sketches.

We may tend to get a false impression of the Auld Licht folk from a cursory perusal of Barrie's writings. It is true that he tries to do them justice and speaks often and again of their sacrifice and devotion, but writing of them after a long passage of years, when he had been schooled to broader views in England, he is apt to dwell on their idiosyncrasies rather than on their strength. The idiosyncrasies, of course, were there; but it might be advisable to trace the causes which produced them.

The founders of the Secession Church broke away from the Establishment because they desired to have a Church which owed allegiance to no one but its Lord. Therefore, the Church which they set up was founded, as far as they knew, on the primitive model of apostolic days. This, more

THE AULD LICHT KIRK—NOW DEMOLISHED

[*Valentine*

than their poverty, was responsible for the unadorned architecture of their buildings. The Auld Licht Kirk in Kirriemuir was a barn-like structure, differing no-wise in its whitewashed exterior from the other buildings in the street. This, however, to Auld Licht eyes, was quite a merit. In apostolic days, the disciples met in one another's houses. Their church was any meeting-place where two or three gathered together to receive the blessing of the Lord. The Auld Lichts, therefore, just looked upon their church building as a meeting-place too. It was the pervading spirit of the Lord that mattered, not the architecture.

In all this they were quite correct. They had got down to fundamentals, and on laying complete stress on the spirit of their worship they built up a vital communion. Unfortunately, in their intense desire for a spiritual supremacy, they were inclined to narrow the content of that spirit. They neglected the influence of the æsthetic factor and also the value of memory and tradition. A church which suggests to us dignity and reverence, and which is also hallowed by memories of the past, gives a gracious content to worship which might be lacking in a more austere building. That was seen in the Auld Licht's character; it was austere and fervent, but it lacked the graces.

It was the same desire to return to the primitive model that led the Auld Lichts to frown upon instrumental music and all exterior aids to worship. " If any man have not the spirit of the Lord, he is none of His." Their worship was the outcome of a personal experience and needed no extraneous aids. Therefore music was barred, and hymns were barred, and written sermons were barred, and written prayers were a thing undreamt of. Their worship must at all costs be held free from the carnal work of man. Spiritual fervour was the only thing that counted. All else was a hindrance and intrusion.

To their main contention we say, " Amen," but we do not feel justified in supporting their conclusions. That music cannot be used to the glory of God, that hymns cannot express a vital spiritual experience, that a written sermon cannot edify, and that men should not make use in worship of the rich liturgy of the past are arguments we cannot allow. These all are means of grace when guided by God's spirit. To neglect them is to limit the expression of our worship. The Auld Lichts, we believe, limited themselves unduly.

The Auld Licht's spiritual experience was narrowed by a failure to trust the spirit. It would lead him into new truth, but, grounding his worship on the model of the past, he did not follow. This reliance on the spirit and failure to trust its leading was both his strength and weakness. It made for fervour, but it hindered development. Yet we must not blame him. It has never been easy for those two aspects of the spiritual life to be harmoniously combined.

Let us now take up the history of the Auld Licht Kirk in Kirriemuir. It was founded in 1775 by certain disaffected burghers. They were not many. When they called their first minister only twenty-nine men signed the call. The minister who took over the pastorate was a Mr.

James Aitken, who was then at the age of twenty-two. He was to shepherd them through sunshine and shadow for fifty-nine long years.

This Mr. Aitken was the original of Mr. Carfrae in *The Little Minister* and was Margaret Ogilvy's pastor. A tall, dignified man (he never walked abroad without his gold-headed cane) he was a faithful minister, and doubtless worthy of the tribute Barrie pays to him in his book. He knew intimately every member of his flock, and many a time must Margaret Ogilvy in her girlhood days have waited in trembling in the kitchen till Mr. Aitken came along to conduct his catechizing. For the good man went from house to house questioning his flock on their knowledge of the Scriptures. Perhaps it was just because his mother was a little old-fashioned in her loyalties that Barrie says a good word for that Shorter Catechism she learned so diligently in her youth. It is something, he says, we learn at the time, not understanding the meaning of it, but the meaning comes long after when we have most need of it. Mr. Aitken, at any rate, built up a strong congregation above the average in knowledge and piety, and among them was Margaret Ogilvy.

The same good minister had many a crisis in the Auld Licht Kirk which seemed nothing more than a local " stushie " at the time, but which was to provide the future novelist with material for his pen. In 1806, in consequence of some trouble with his elders, he came to loggerheads with the Presbytery. He had deposed two men from office, since they refused to give up to him the key of the box which held the cash and title-deeds. The Presbytery ordered him to reinstate them.

He refused, and they deposed him in his turn.

This is the split to which Barrie refers in the beginning of his sketch of the Auld Licht Kirk in *Auld Licht Idylls*. Mr. Aitken was in no wise daunted, and taking the majority of his congregation with him, carried on his ministrations on the common. At length a new church was built in Bank Street, to which Mr. Aitken and his trusty flock returned. This was the building in which Margaret Ogilvy worshipped.

But even in this new church harmony was not restored. The closing year of Mr. Aitken's life was embittered by a controversy which threatened again to rend the church in two. There was no instrumental music in the church, of course, and it was the practice for the precentor to lead the praise. This he did in a fashion which would now seem to us intolerable, but which was a concession to the ignorance of the times. Instead of singing a psalm right through either from memory or with the assistance of the psalter, the congregation sung each line after it had been read over by the precentor. He would read, or intone, a line and they would sing it. He would read another and they would sing it, and so on to the end. The procedure now proposed was that the precentor should read the psalm, and that the congregation should sing it through. It was an innovation and strenuously resisted. One old lady showed her total disapproval of this new-fangled worship by refusing to enter church for the opening psalm and by rising and going out at every item of praise. Barrie refers to her in *Auld Licht Idylls*. The old lady's cantrips were also remembered by Dr.

Whyte, of " Free St. George's," who recalled the joy with which small boys gathered round the door and waited for her exit and re-entrance.

The Rev. Mr. Aitken died in 1834, and the minister of the Auld Licht Kirk in Barrie's day was the Rev. Robert Craig. He was a preacher and pastor of the very highest order, but Barrie knew little about him. It was James Aitken of his mother's days who lingered in his memory. He, if any, is not only Mr. Carfrae, but also the Little Minister himself, combined in the latter case, one must say, with some of Barrie's own qualities. His dynamics in the pulpit, his fervour in pastoral visitation, his catechizing and his zeal for souls—all are Mr. Aitken's. His height . . . But we shall say nothing about his height. Gavin Dishart did not like it.

BARRIE'S BIRTH AND
EARLY YEARS

BARRIE'S BIRTH AND EARLY YEARS

IF we would bridge the gulf that lies between the handloom weaving days and the Kirriemuir of to-day, we shall do it very neatly by turning to *Margaret Ogilvy*. There in the second chapter Barrie tells us of the change that took place before his very eyes. " Before I reached my tenth year," he says, " a giant entered my native place in the night, and we woke to find him in possession. He transformed it into a new town at a rate with which we boys only could keep up, for as fast as he built dams we made rafts to sail in them; he knocked down houses, and there we were crying ' Pilly! ' among the ruins; he dug trenches, and we jumped them; we had to be dragged by the legs from beneath his engines; he sunk wells and in we went. But although there were never circumstances to which boys could not adapt themselves in half an hour, older folks are slower in the uptake, and I am sure they stood and gaped at the changes so suddenly being worked in our midst, and scarcely knew their way home now in the dark. Where had been formerly but the click of the shuttle was soon the roar of ' power,' handlooms were pushed into a corner as a room is cleared for a dance; every morning at half-past five the town was wakened with a yell, and from a chimney-stack that rose high into our caller air the conqueror waved for evermore his flag of smoke. Another

Barrie's parents were working-folk; but they were ambitious for their sons. Before young James was born they had an elder son, Alex, preparing to go to college. And go to college he did, and proved a very brilliant student. He went to Aberdeen University in 1858 with Alexander Whyte. Between them they hired a room, paying for their lodgings three shillings and sixpence per week, and he graduated four years later with first-class honours in Classics. We can imagine the pride of his hard-working father and mother. Little did they dream of another son who was to make his elder brother's eminence seem small. James at the time of his brother's graduation was two years old.

Our Author was born in 1860 in the little tenement house that stands on the Brechin Road. It is a working-class locality nowadays, and it was so then, but when we look at its dingy exterior, we must remember that more than seventy years have come and gone since Barrie's parents came to stay there. The neighbours were handloom weavers, and from every open door and window came the click-clack, click-clack of the looms. But in the morning of the 9th of May the noise of the looms was suspended for an hour or two. The neighbours had gone in to see Margaret Ogilvy's little boy.

It was a poor home into which that baby came. Every penny had to be earned and therefore every penny counted. Well might the busy mother economize all she could, for there were many mouths to feed. (There was a family of ten in all, but some died when very young.) Clothes, seemingly past repair, were coaxed by gentle hands to

BARRIE'S BIRTHPLACE

do duty for another season. Woe betide the
youngster who refused to wear his elder brother's
cast-off " breeks "! Food was wholesome, but it
was often just the outcome of a penny bone and
something from the garden. " Take porridge for
breakfast, or else you go without!" Yet Margaret
Ogilvy had a son at college and was already determined that she would send another.

At the " poopit-fit " of the South Free Church
Barrie was baptized. No clandestine christening at
home for the saintly Daniel Cormick. The famous
christening robe was again produced and " borne
magnificently (*something inside it now*[1]) down the
aisle to the pulpit-side, when a stir of expectancy
went through the church and we kicked each
other's feet beneath the book-board but were
reverent in the face; and however the child might
behave, laughing brazenly or skirling to its mother's
shame, and whatever the father as he held it up
might do, look doited probably or bow at the
wrong time, the christening robe of long experience helped him through." So writes Barrie in
Margaret Ogilvy, and so was it done to him.

The first six years, he says, are all a blank. At
the end of that period he commenced his schooling
at the private school of the Misses Adam in Bank
Street. This genteel seminary of infant learning
he has celebrated to all the world as " The Hanky
School " of *Sentimental Tommy*. It was kept by
two maiden ladies, the Miss Ailie and Miss Kitty
of the story, whose father, a retired clergyman,
had come to stay in Kirriemuir. Here Barrie was
taught the rudiments under a rule that differed
somewhat from the discipline of " The Dovecot,"

[1] The italics only are ours.

in that it was strict as it was kindly. The "tawse" were forbidden, but a stout ruler administered correction when required. One other punishment, much favoured by the delinquents, was detention in the coal-hole. The most desired of all was to suffer splendid isolation on the lobby stairs outside. For here there was a chance that the Rev. Mr. Adam would pass and relieve the tedium of waiting with the gift of a peppermint drop. Barrie was often on the stairs.

After learning his "A B C's" with the Misses Adam, young James was transferred to the Free Church School, where he received the usual elementary education. He was a lively little sprite. One of his old companions, Mr. James Robb of Kirriemuir, who is still his closest friend, tells of one ploy with a "chickie mailie." This was made out of a button attached by a string to a pin. The pin was stuck in the sash of a window so that the button was suspended against the glass. Then by means of another *long* string (the length depended on the perpetrator's courage) the button could be made to tap, tap, tap against the window-pane. Barrie, of course, describes the prank in *Sentimental Tommy*. There to the house of the Painted Lady came "certain big fellows with a turnip lantern." They employ the "chickie mailie" on her window and make her scream. "Big fellows with a lantern," he writes. We can almost see his lips curl in virtuous indignation. He is not the only preacher who declaims against the follies of his youth!

Perhaps we might lift the curtain on a dark past a very little further. One evening in the gloaming a worthy bailie of Kirriemuir wended his way homewards along the Brechin Road. In the centre of the road he saw a parcel. Like a good citizen, he picked it up and carefully examined it. Then he tucked it under his arm and proceeded on his way. He had not gone far, however, when it was jerked from his arm by some unseen power. The string which did the trick was in the hands of —Peter Pan.

On another occasion Barrie and some schoolmates set out to visit the folk of Tannadice, a nearby village. In a courtesy call like this, of course, they had to be dressed up " in their braws." This they effected very easily by turning their jackets inside out. Their good intentions, however, were not fully appreciated by the Tannadice boys. They imagined, somehow, that these strangers were showing off. The deputation from Kirriemuir retreated, jackets right side out, returning their showers of stones.

All of which goes to show that the creator of " Sentimental Tommy " and " Peter Pan " was just a natural boy.

Like any other natural boy, Barrie was fond of sport. Cricket was his favourite. How could it be otherwise when the Hill of Kirriemuir, he assures us, is the finest cricket pitch in all the world? To substantiate that opinion, he has just presented it with a pavilion worthy of the site. But in the olden days there was no pavilion—just the level sward of turf and the grandeur of the Grampians beyond. The game was played with a home-made bat. The wicket was a flat boulder set on end. Flannels were unknown, and a jacket turned inside out marked a fielder from a mere looker-on. The ball might be a hard one to-day and a soft one to-morrow, but the *game* was the thing. That game to Barrie is almost sacred. He has written a book on cricket. It is not published.

His leanings towards literature and the stage were evident as a boy. The first book he ever read was *Robinson Crusoe* and, oh, how eagerly he read it ! It was followed by *The Arabian Nights*. But that statement must be qualified. The *Nights* was dipped into but never read. Both he and his mother were deceived in it when they borrowed it from the library. They thought they were Knights, and on discovering they were Nights they put it back. The next idol of his fancy was the *Pilgrim's Progress*. He was fascinated by that book. Even the garden was turned into a Slough of Despond, to the consternation of his mother. He read every book he could beg or borrow, buying one—now and again. Thus began that education which came to *Auld Licht Idylls*, *The Little Minister*, and *Mary Rose*.

In the house presided over by David Barrie, the theatre was not a place to be mentioned, far less visited. In truth there was little opportunity, though travelling shows, with their tumblers, jugglers, sword-swallowers and the rest, came to Kirriemuir twice a year to whet a young lad's appetite for the world of motley. There, whether he had the money for his admission or whether he had it not, young Barrie contrived to make himself aware of all that was going on. Not only so, but the boys held shows among themselves—admission " three preens " or a " bool "—and in a house in Bank Street, over a shop which Barrie haunted, for it was the only book-shop in Kirriemuir, in a back

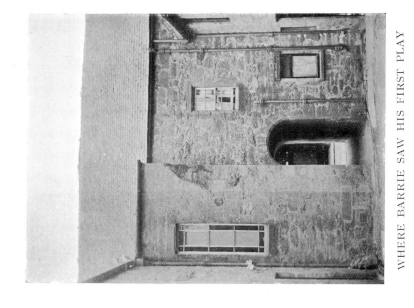

WHERE BARRIE SAW HIS FIRST PLAY

BARRIE'S HOME IN FORFAR

bedroom on the upper floor, he saw his first play. It was only a boy's affair. The stage was the bed and the actors were puppets, but it was the beginning—of the end.

Another prank in which Barrie was concerned might be mentioned because he refers to it himself in his introduction to *Peter Pan*. Before the house in which he was born there stands a washing-house. It is not a very pretentious affair—eight feet by six we should say it will be. Here the boys of the neighbourhood used to foregather to conduct their ploys. One of these was a play written and acted in by our youthful hero, of which the culminating act consisted of trying to put each other in the washing-house boiler. That was at seven or thereabouts, but early impressions stick, and when Barrie had to find a house for Wendy in the Never Never Land in *Peter Pan*, it was to this old wash-house his mind went back. The only difference, he says, is that " it never wore John's hat for a chimney." " Lum " hats in Thrums were put to much more sacred uses!

The washing-house and Barrie's birthplace were in the market in 1928, and an enterprising American wanted to buy them and carry them off to the States. Another argument for Stephen Leacock, who avers that soon if we Britishers want to see our national treasures we shall need to cross the Atlantic! Happily we have been saved the journey this time, for the property has been bought by Major A. D. Lauder of London, who means to endow them both and leave them in Kirriemuir.

The events of which we have been writing all happened before Barrie was eight years old. At eight he moved to Glasgow to the care of his brother Alex, who was Classical Master at the Glasgow Academy. Barrie remembers well the smoky city of the West, if only for one significant reason. There was a horse show in the Glasgow Academical's ground and he patronized it. He lost a penny in the ground, and in going back at night to look for it he found a threepenny bit. He has never forgotten that day !

In the meantime, while young James was achieving both wealth and learning in Glasgow, events were moving in Kirriemuir. The altered mode of production of jute cloth had changed his father's circumstances. Handloom weaving was going out and power-loom weaving was coming rapidly to the fore. David Barrie, seeing he must make some change under the changed conditions, gave up his handlooms and went down to be a clerk with Messrs. Laird, whose new works had just opened in the town of Forfar. Young James arrived home in time to assist at the removal.

Triumphant on the top of a cart of furniture, he rumbled down the road that leads to Zoar and the Tilliedrum of his stories.

SCHOOLDAYS IN FORFAR

SCHOOLDAYS IN FORFAR

FORFAR also had undergone the change from a handloom-weaving to a factory town. The change was to bring about a greater prosperity and, incidentally, a decreased population. It was to share in this prosperity that David Barrie came down South. The new position meant an increase in his income, and he took residence with his wife and family in a fairly substantial house in Canmore Street. The house still stands, surrounded by a high stone wall which includes a garden. Here it must have been that, fired by the *Pilgrim's Progress*, the youthful Barrie created his Slough of Despond to the consternation of his mother, for the house in Kirriemuir had no garden. And on the drying green under Malcolm Canmore's hill, with his *Chatterbox* or *Coral Island* laid aside, he lay and built his castles in the air. Whether the historic site fired his imagination we cannot say. At least he found himself living over a site which had witnessed the coming of Queen Margaret, and had known the besieging of the English and the wrath of Robert the Bruce. For he it was who destroyed the castle when harrying the English out of the country before the battle of Bannockburn. At any rate the future novelist was living on ground which might fire the most sterile imagination. But his heart was not in history. It was in Margaret Ogilvy's Thrums.

The house in which he was living was small, but commodious compared with the house in Brechin Road. There was a kitchen and a bedroom downstairs and another bedroom and " best " room upstairs, with a little crooked wooden stair leading up to them. By reason of modern alterations, the house has been greatly changed since Barrie's day. The old ivy has been taken from the walls, which have been reinforced by a covering of cement; the outside stairs which once adorned it have gone, while the internal alterations have been numerous. The house still stands, however, a memorial of a time when an ambitious youngster received his education in the county town, and played about its closes.

The Barries were staunch Church supporters, and when they settled in Forfar they immediately became members of the East Free Church, situated in the Back Wynd, not a hundred yards from where they lived. Unfortunately the Communion Roll which would mark the precise dates of their coming to and going from the town is nowhere to be found, but the record of the contributors to the Sustentation Fund reveals the fact that David Barrie and his family contributed with the utmost regularity from May, 1870, till February, 1872. No purpose is to be served in publishing private giving, but we may mention, in David Barrie's honour, that his contributions were generous for his station in life. Old members of the church can still remember him, and Margaret Ogilvy and Jane Ann and James, coming to church Sunday by Sunday to take their seat on the

BARRIE AS A SCHOOLBOY
(First on Left in Front Row)

minister's left. Is this the church of happy memory where a boy came in, lifting his feet high, to let folk see he had new boots on?

James was sent to Forfar Academy to continue his education. His days there, except to one or two, have almost been forgotten, but a very fortunate incident brings them back again. One day, when the school was in progress, a travelling photographer called, pushing his line of business. The master was willing, and the pupils, junior and senior, left their classes with a " whoop " and flocked to the back door. Barrie was among the junior lot, and very solemnly he sat down to have his photograph taken. On page 64 there is a copy of that famous picture. Barrie is seated in the front row first from the left. The blue bonnets of the boys and the tall hats of the masters seem rather incongruous to-day. They were *de rigueur* fifty years ago.

Some interesting reminiscences are still preserved of Barrie's days in Forfar. " He was a shy, sensitive lad," it has been stated, " and was not over fond of athletics, but a keen lover of the country." We question the statement that he was not fond of athletics. He may not have been *good* at them, but he was *fond* of them. We wish he would publish that book on cricket.

Like any other laddie he had an eye for mischief. The following might be related as characteristic of him.

One Saturday afternoon he and a friend had gone for a country walk. (A " cookie " each and a penny to buy milk comprised the commissariat.) Now they had gone for a walk, but there was no reason why they *should* walk if Providence were kind. Providence, on this occasion, smiled on them, and soon an old, ramshackle cart drawn by a struggling pony came rattling along their way. It was weighted by two farmer bodies whose avoirdupois suggested expansiveness if not positive good nature. At any rate, Barrie took heart of grace and besought accommodation for " twa puir laddies with a long way to go," and soon found himself and his companion adding to the burden of the pony. They reached their objective all right with the overpowering satisfaction—there could be none greater to a Scottish boy—of having achieved " a hurl for nothing."

Barrie at school possessed a charming wistfulness, and even then his aptitude for acquiring and storing knowledge was remarkable. He was particularly good at evolving stories. From two sources we learn of authentic occasions where he charmed his schoolfellows with the products of his fancy. One old schoolfellow at Kirriemuir tells of how at " minutes " he took a privileged few aside to reveal to them the secret of a coming play. At Forfar his tales were of *Ivanhoe* or *Martin Rattler*. His fertile imagination, then, is not a legend. It was to develop afterwards in the manner that we know.

Forfar, as we have seen, is the Tilliedrum of his stories. There is as much Forfar as Kirriemuir in many of them, for they were both handloom-weaving towns with the same fashions and traditions. One incident which concerns them both is well worth repetition, if only because Barrie makes so much of it, in different vein, in his *Auld Licht Idylls*. We refer to the battle of Cabbylatch, fought over Tammas Lunan's body. The reader

66

will remember that Barrie's version of the fray is that Tammas Lunan died in Forfar, that the Forfarians brought the body to the Parish Boundary, but refused to move one step farther in the direction of Kirriemuir. The Kirriemarians came to their boundary to receive it, but when the two opposing parties met, they differed as to where the boundary line was to be drawn. Neither side would budge an inch. Stones were thrown which required to be avenged, and the battle of Cabbylatch was the result.

The historical version is somewhat different. Between Forfar and Kirriemuir, in the district known as Ballinshoe, there was a bit of common ground known as Muir's Moss. The ownership of this common ground was disputed between the sutors[1] of Forfar and the weavers of Kirriemuir. They determined to fight it out between them, and an organized battle was the result. The Forfarians were defeated, and the injury to their pride has hardly been forgiven even to the present day. It gave rise to the following lines :

" *The Kirriemarians and the Forfarians*
  Met at Muir Moss,
The Kirriemarians beat the Forfarians
  Back to the Cross;
Sutors ye are, and sutors ye'll be,
Fie upon Forfar! Kirriemuir bears the gree."

Barrie had heard of the incident, and an everfertile imagination supplied the rest!

[1] Shoemakers. Shoemaking was at one time Forfar's staple industry.

THE DISCOVERY OF THRUMS

IN February, 1872, Barrie's father left Forfar to return to Kirriemuir. Although he was now in his fifty-eighth year, he had secured further promotion as chief clerk at Messrs. Stewart & Ogilvy's, a new factory which had just been founded by the banks of the Gairie. He took up residence in " Strathview," a commodious dwelling-house at the junction of the Glamis and Forfar roads, facing a little whitewashed cottage on the brae. We may be sure he never gave a thought to this cottage at the time, but it was to make his son famous, becoming known to all the world as " The Cottage on the Brae."

In " Strathview " David Barrie and Margaret Ogilvy and the gentle Jane Ann settled for the remainder of their days. It is only an old stone building with its back to the front like that tenement in the Brechin Road, but Barrie casts around it the glamour of his genius. Here took place the final scenes of *Margaret Ogilvy*. No traveller can pass it by, for all its drab exterior, without thinking of that " gey auld farrant heroine," as she would call herself in mild dispraise and all her gentle ways. We are grateful to Barrie, and always shall be, that he remembered that all of us, deep down in our hearts, love goodness, and so opened the door of that humble home and let us peep inside.

So young James had again to change his domicile and his schooling. Barrie, the man, has never been a great traveller. Perhaps he got it all over in his younger days, for here he was, returning to Kirriemuir at the age of twelve, having been as far afield as Glasgow and having lived for almost two years in the alien town of Forfar. But his journeyings were only beginning; for he had an uncle in Motherwell, the Rev. David Ogilvy, his mother's only brother and minister of the Dalziel Free Church there. Hither James seems to have gone for the rest of the year 1872, though he may have put in a spell at Webster's Seminary, the High School of Kirriemuir. (Mr. Ramsay MacDonald, in a rather vague reference in a speech, speaks of his being there.) At any rate, his estrangement from regular schooling was only temporary, for, as Mr. J. A. Hammerton tells us in his *Barrie*, he became a scholar in Dumfries Academy in the autumn session of 1873. The reason for his going so far southward as Dumfries is not far to seek. His brother Alex, classical master in the Glasgow Academy, had just been appointed Inspector of Schools for Dumfries and district, so James was again taken under his wing to complete his education.

His literary development proceeded apace in Dumfries. In the town there was an old book-shop run by Mr. Anderson, brother of Sir James Anderson, captain of the *Great Eastern*, which laid the first Atlantic cable. There was an attic above it where old books and stores were kept, and here the budding author, friendly with the proprietor, browsed to his heart's content. What serious literature he read, we know not. We may surmise he read Carlyle. He saw the great man many a time taking his solitary walk along the country roads, but he was afraid to speak to him. Shyness was natural on Barrie's part and taciturnity just as natural on Carlyle's. The lighter literature, however, provided by Ballantyne, Marryat and Fenimore Cooper he devoured.

His first adventure in authorship was his contribution to a school paper edited by Wellwood Anderson, the son of the friendly bookseller. It was called *The Clown*, and was written in the vein of schoolboy humour. Barrie contributed the " Reckollections of a Schoolmaster " edited by James Barrie, M.A., A.S.S., LL.D. Little did he think that the recollections of a schoolmaster were to make him famous. It was the dominie of Glen Quharity, writing down the " short and simple annals of the poor," who was to reveal that James Barrie, M.A., LL.D., as he afterwards became, was not an A.S.S.

But it was playwriting that brought him notoriety in Dumfries. Young Wellwood, his friend, on a visit to Edinburgh, had seen a play " Off the Line " which had fired his fancy. He was President of the Dumfries Amateur Dramatic Society and Barrie was Secretary, so between them they agreed to produce a plagiarized version of the play. It was preceded by a curtain raiser, " Bandelero the Bandit," a play of the swashbuckler type of which Barrie himself was the author. The production of the plays had dire results, for a local clergyman, who evidently desired a monopoly of the " blood and thunder " of the town, tried to have it banned. Professor Blackie was drawn into the controversy with highly diverting results. We quote the incident as it is written by one of Barrie's contemporaries at the school.

" One thinks of Barrie's first attempt at play-writing, ' Off the Line,' which was produced in the Christmas holidays of the session 1876-7, under the patronage of the masters. It aroused the ire of a stern old United Presbyterian minister who was a member of the School Board, and who at its next meeting gave vent to his feelings and protested against such a thing being allowed in the school. He declared that though he had neither seen nor read the play it was ' immoral,' because he under-stood that in it were ' two awful villains ' ! This led to a paper-war in the local journals. Somehow the reverend gentleman dragged in the name of Professor Blackie. Shortly afterwards the vivacious Professor came to lecture in the Mechanics' Hall in support of his pet scheme of establishing a Gaelic Chair in Edinburgh University, for which, by the way, he said ' Her Majesty, decent woman, has given £20.' But as he strode up and down the platform, he launched forth about ' the storm in a tea-cup ' and invited the minister—who, however, was not present, though members of his family were—to come on to the platform and he would ' pound him to a jelly.' "

Thus Barrie learned, early in his career, the value of a free advertisement.

One other play he wrote in Dumfries was called " The Weavers." It is noteworthy because of a certain incident which graced his personal appear-ance as Adele. Adele was a damsel and (forgive us !) radiant with beauty. So much so that when the play was performed on one occasion a member of the audience fell in love with her and asked to be introduced. The *venue* of the performance was the Crichton Mental Institution. So they say, at any rate.

After five years at Dumfries Academy young Barrie proceeded to Edinburgh University, where he was further confirmed in his love for literature by the great English master—Masson. His first sight of Masson, he informs us in *An Edinburgh Eleven*, was specially impressive. " It was the opening of the session when the fees were paid, and a whisper ran round the quadrangle that Masson had set off home with three hundred one-pound notes stuffed into his trouser pockets. There was a solemn swell of awe-struck students to the gates, and some of us could not help following him. He took his pockets coolly. When he stopped it was at a second-hand book-stall where he rummaged for a long time. Eventually he pounced upon a dusty, draggled little volume, and went off proudly with it beneath his arm. He seemed to look suspiciously at strangers now, but it was not the money but the book he was keeping guard over. His pockets, however, were unmistakably bulging out. I resolved to go in for literature."

Making all allowances for Barrie's facetiousness, we may be sure that Masson did influence him deeply in his love for literature, and had more than a little to do with turning his thoughts from the law, to study which he had gone up to the University. Perhaps he influenced him also in another way just as important. " Lecturing on

Barrie's mind was broadening that he discovered
Thrums.

Encouraged by his success in *The St. James's
Gazette*, he gave up his position in Nottingham and
went down to London to try his hand at free-lance
journalism. It was a hazardous thing to do, and
he " scorned delights and lived laborious days " for
four long years. But he was happy in making the
friendship of one or two influential men, who
recognized merit when they saw it. Alexander
Riach of the *Daily Telegraph* gave him a hand,
then W. Robertson Nicoll of the *British Weekly*.
The latter advised him to publish some of his
sketches. He found him a publisher for *Auld
Licht Idylls*. The book was produced in April,
1888, and its author sprang into fame.

It is interesting, at this time of the day, to look
over some of the first Press notices that greeted
Auld Licht Idylls. The *Spectator* said, " At once
the most successful, the most truly literary, and
the most realistic attempt that has been made for
years, if not for generations, to reproduce humble
Scottish life. . . . We have thought it positively
our duty to call attention at some length to this
book, because in its fidelity to truth, its humour
and its vivid interest, it is a complete and welcome
contrast to the paltry ' duds ' which are nowadays
printed by the dozen as pictures of humble and
religious life in Scotland."

The Academy said, " Not only the best book
dealing exclusively with Scotch humble life, but
the only book of the kind, deserving to be classed
as literature, that has been published for at least a
quarter of a century."

The Athenæum said, " Very graphic is the

description of the storm-beaten, snow-laden clachan of grey stones, and bright is the observant insight displayed by the solitary and philosophic dominie who tells the tale."

We imagine that Frederick Greenwood and W. Robertson Nicoll and J. M. Barrie would be pleased.

THE THRUMS LITERATURE

IN the changed circumstances which the success
of *Auld Licht Idylls* brought him Barrie was
now able to leave London and make long stays in
Kirriemuir. His parents, we remember, were now
settled in " Strathview," where there was ample
peace and accommodation for their literary son.
Barrie was anxious to be beside his mother, not only
because of his love for her, but because he desired
material for his books. This material he often had
to fish from her with the dexterity of an angler.
" We always spoke to each other in broad Scotch,"
he says, " but now and again she would use a word
that was new to me, or I might hear one of her
contemporaries use it. Now is my opportunity to
angle for its meaning. If I ask boldly what
was that word she used just now, something like
' bilbie ' or ' silvendy '? she blushes and says that
she never said anything so common, or hoots! it
is some auld-farrant word about which she can tell
me nothing. But if in the course of conversation
I remark casually, ' Did he find bilbie? ' or ' Was
that quite silvendy? ' (though the sense of the
question is vague to me) she falls into the trap,
and the words explain themselves in her replies."
It was from Margaret Ogilvy he culled the dialect
which was so quickly passing and which he uses so
naturally in his books. It is from her also, as we

have seen, that he obtained many of his stories of old-time Kirriemuir.

Of course, the Kirriemuir which Barrie knew and the Kirriemuir of which his mother told him melted into one another. He himself in his boyhood days had listened to the click-clack, click-clack, thud-thud of the handloom, and knew many of the old handloom weavers by name and reputation. Even when he came back to Kirriemuir there were still some old handloom workers left, too old to go into the factories. By his careful observation of what was left and his vivid imagination of what had gone before, he was able to reproduce their lives. That he did not caricature these men whose lives he set out to chronicle is evident from the words of Dr. Alexander Whyte, who knew them well. " All of us in the town," says the doctor, " know the characters Mr. Barrie describes, and had taken them and their eccentricities just as a complete part of our town life, scarcely worth notice. But when a man of genius put them into print that made all the difference. The Kirriemuir people were beyond the average for shrewdness and intelligence. Some of the working men were deeply read in literature and philosophy. Mr. Barrie has thoroughly grasped the characters of the little community, with all their humour and pathos. ' Thrums ' is a true picture of my native place."

It is as well to take note of that verdict, as it is sometimes asserted that Barrie sentimentalized the place out of all recognition and caricatured the people as characters in his books. We must remember that the old Scots character was very strongly marked, especially in out-of-the-way places, and he who had an eye for men's foibles in Kirriemuir and " there awa' " had rich material for his pen. But Kirriemuir was not unique in that. There were worthies in Forfar and in many another Scottish town who could have sprung to life in inimitable humour had they had a Barrie as their chronicler.

At the same time, it should be remembered that Barrie was a writer and not an historian. His interest first and foremost was human nature and its various manifestations. He was out to interest and to win the public. There is a passage in *The Life of Walter Page* which might well describe his outlook. There that shrewd editor and ambassador says, " When you wish to win a man to do what *you* want him to do, you take along a few well-established facts, some reasoning and such-like, but you also take along three or four or five parts of human nature—kindliness, courtesy and such things—sympathy and a human touch."

Barrie wished to win the public to buy his books. So he left out all in which the public was not interested, and concentrated on kindliness, courtesy, sympathy and the human touch. If this tends to give us a one-sided view of Kirriemuir we must remember he had no alternative. The public was not interested in the steady-going Moderates of the Auld Kirk or even in the monthly " rumpus " at the Council meeting, but it was interested in the idiosyncrasies of the Auld Lichts. They represented human nature.

It was this interest in human nature that kept Barrie back from describing scenery. Of course, for a large part of his time he was resident in London, and a first-hand description of natural sights was quite impossible. And perhaps he took the beauty of his countryside for granted. But he knew that the large mass of the reading public was not vitally interested in descriptions of nature. It was not but what he could do it well when he chose. The opening page of *The Little Minister* has as good a piece of descriptive writing as one could wish to see. " It was the time of year when the ground is carpeted beneath the firs with brown needles, when split nuts patter all day from the beech, and children lay yellow corn on the dominie's desk to remind him that now they are needed in the fields. The day was so silent that carts could be heard rumbling a mile away." He did not choose to exercise that power however. His interest was in men and particularly in what we would term nowadays " the psychological study of men." If he could reveal the pathos and sublimity of common life he was quite content.

This leads to carelessness in detailed descriptions of Kirriemuir. The House on the Brae and the Auld Licht Manse one, of course, could recognize at a glance, but there are other places where he plays ducks and drakes with his material. He invents a mythical double-dykes at the coffin brig, presumably to bring in the story of a convivial farmer who, when returning home in the evening, was grateful for their assistance. The real double-dykes in Kirriemuir is on the other side of the Hill, half a mile away. The Schoolhouse in the Glen of *The Little Minister* he brings to within five miles of Thrums, though its actual distance is nearer ten. There are other instances, which we shall notice later on, of this rough handling of his material. As we have said, he was not an historian. He was an author writing for a public which, as far as those small matters were concerned, did not care a rap.

We may surmise that in some instances also he deliberately manipulated his localities. In this he was very wise. Was there not an Earl at the Spittal whom he treated rather roughly? In weaving a story around his native place he had to guard against his fiction being taken for literal truth. Even so, in his sketches and novels Barrie has been faithful to the main features of Kirriemuir and district, and he who visits the town to-day may find himself, without much difficulty, walking in his footsteps.

THE EARLY THRUMS SKETCHES

THE EARLY THRUMS SKETCHES

T HE visitor to Kirriemuir to-day will probably
experience a feeling of disappointment. He
has pictured it as a sleepy little hamlet,
dominated by an Auld Licht Kirk and an Auld
Licht Manse, with its outstanding feature a whitewashed cottage on a brae. He finds that the
Auld Licht Kirk has gone, the Manse is hidden
behind an array of modern villas, the cottage on
the brae is a modern dwelling-house, beautified
by shrubs and flowers. His greatest disappointment will be the town itself. Where are the
outside stairs, and the winding closes, and the
Den and the Glens and all that Barrie wrote about
so bonnily? They are all there, but it needs
time and trouble to find them out. There is no
good in turning away impatiently and saying,
" We have been deceived. This is a modern
country town and a busy one at that." Just start
to explore a little, and all that Barrie wrote about
comes back.

We must, of course, remember that he idealized
a bit, and a good bit too. He is sometimes even
himself afraid that he excites our hopes too high.
He reminds us in *Sentimental Tommy* that the
Marywell Brae is " gey an' mean an' bleak."
He protests that he has thought too much of the
outside stairs. He has even been tempted to

boast too strongly of the Den. We allow him the latitude of his genius, but the place itself is worthy. It is not too mean and it is not too bleak. There is old-time treasure in its closes and its wynds; the Den is still a centre of romance where lads and lasses stroll; the glens are very beautiful clad in their summer verdure or covered by the snow; the view from the Hill, we declare without fear of contradiction, is one of the most wonderful in Scotland. It was not a *tour de force* on the part of Barrie when he wrote about the beauties of his Thrums.

The way to know Thrums, as Barrie would reveal her, is to go over the different districts he treats of in his books. For our author selected his material, and after writing of one locality, turned his attention to another. The local setting of *A Window in Thrums* differs from that of *The Little Minister*, and that again from *Sentimental Tommy*. It is only in *Auld Licht Idylls* that he treated of Thrums as a whole. Then he was giving a series of impressionistic sketches. He was only discovering his field. When he found that the public was interested in it, he began to exercise economy in the use of his material. So if we would know Thrums, we had better explore her gradually as Barrie reveals her bit by bit in the succession of his novels.

First of all, let us look at Thrums through the medium of the *Auld Licht Idylls*. Indeed no better introduction to her could be given than Barrie's first notice of her in that book. It is of an old-time Thrums he writes, the town of Margaret Ogilvy. " Thrums," he says, " is the name I give here to the handful of houses jumbled

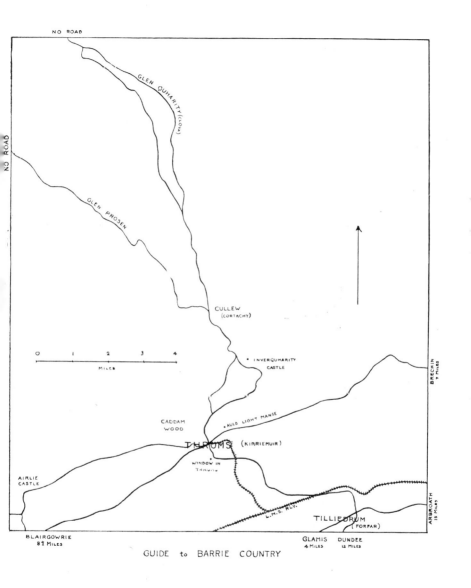

NO ROAD

NO ROAD

GLEN QUHARITY (CLOVA)

GLEN PROSEN

CULLEW
(CORTACHY)

INVERQUHARITY
CASTLE

CADDAM
WOOD

AULD LIGHT MANSE

THRUMS (KIRRIEMUIR)

WINDOW IN
THRUMS

AIRLIE
CASTLE

L.M.S. RLY.

TILLIEDRUM
(FORFAR)

BRECHIN
7 MILES

ARBROATH
15 MILES

0   1   2   3   4
MILES

BLAIRGOWRIE
8¾ MILES

GLAMIS
4 MILES

DUNDEE
12 MILES

GUIDE to BARRIE COUNTRY

together in a cup, which is the town nearest the schoolhouse. Until twenty years ago its every other room, earthen-floored and showing the rafters overhead, had a handloom, and hundreds of weavers lived and died Thoreaus ' ben the hoose ' without knowing it. In those days the cup overflowed and left several houses on the top of the Hill, where their cold skeletons still stand. The road that climbs from the square, which is Thrums' heart, to the north is so steep and straight, that in a sharp frost children hunker at the top and are blown down with a roar and a rush on rails of ice. At such times, when viewed from the cemetery where his traveller from the schoolhouse gets his first glimpse of the little town, Thrums is but two church steeples and a dozen red patches standing out of a snow heap." That is an accurate description as far as it goes. But it is only an impression of what Thrums looks like from the Hill. Once the traveller has come inside the town he will realize that it *is* a town and not a little hamlet.

Its outstanding feature is the square, " which is Thrums' heart," and therefore the visitor will not have much difficulty in finding it. It is two minutes' walk from the railway station and now-adays 'buses from north, south, east and west deposit their passengers in it. It is somewhat changed from Barrie's day. In his time the streets which converged upon it had each a house in the centre of them, so that the stranger who found himself in the square found himself wonder-ing how he was to get out and presently how he got in. Robert Louis Stevenson, who was once in Thrums on a fishing pilgrimage, described it very aptly in a letter he wrote to Barrie as a haphazard group of houses " squeezed round that square like chickens clustering round a hen." To-day, with the removal of some of the houses, that aspect of it has changed. But the old town house is still standing, blocking up one of the entrances, leaving only a bottle-necked exit to the south. It was all like that in Barrie's day.

The town house itself is the great place of interest in the square. It used to be the town prison and the seat of authority of the Ogilvys, who were responsible for justice in the district. Its former glories have departed and it now houses a chemist's shop, but a little imagination is all that is needed to turn it into the building where Babbie the Egyptian played her pranks and Snecky the Bellman delivered his proclamations. Babbie the Egyptian every reader of Barrie will remember, but Snecky the Bellman might be overlooked. He is mentioned in *Auld Licht Idylls*, and had all the importance of an officer of the law. " His proclamations were provided by those who employed him, but his soul was his own. Having cried a potato roup, he would sometimes add a word of warning, such as, ' I wudna advise ye, lads, to hae onything to do wi' thae tatties; they're diseased.' Once, just before the cattle market, he was sent round by the local laird to announce that any drover taking the short cut through the grounds of Muckle Plowy would be prosecuted to the utmost limits of the law. The people were aghast. ' Hoots, lads,' Snecky said, ' dinna fash yoursels. It's juist a haver o' the grieve's.' " Snecky was drawn from life. The original was Tam Barnett, who was town-crier, policeman, general messenger, and the trusty ally of all the school children of the district. He used to plead with the masters on special days for a holiday for the bairns. Barrie has probably immortalized him out of gratitude.

The old town house itself has a history worthy of its place in the centre of the township. Built by the Ogilvys to keep a hold on the inhabitants of the town, it has seen many a stormy passage in the life of Kirriemuir. The town was governed by a Baron Bailie, the local representative of the chief, and sometimes his government was anything but just, as the following extract shows. It is taken from a document headed " Reasons of Advocation, Declinature or Appeal," and was prepared by James Ogilvy of Kirriemuir against the Bailie and his depute on the 20th July, 1733. Here is a catalogue of the Bailie's crimes :

" He apprehends poor people without a written warrant and sends them to prison without a writ assigning the cause of it.

" His way of apprehending is—he comes at midnight with his depute, his clerk and others, armed with guns, pistols, swords ; breaks open their doors and hales man and wife to prison.

" When they are in prison he sends in people to flatter and threaten to give him money, or bill for money, before sentence or trial.

" If the prisoners consent not or refuse to accuse themselves, he shuts them up in the low prison, terrifies them with threatenings, and sets needless guards at strong prison doors.

" Sometimes he refuses bail, and when he

admits to bail he obliges poor people to find bail for exorbitant sums, such as a thousand merks, or a hundred pounds sterling.

" He obliges poor people to pay exorbitant sums or fees to the clerk for bail bonds almost every court day, and pay exorbitant for them.

" He detains some in prison several days, sometimes several weeks, and when they will not give money nor accuse themselves, dismisses them without trial or sentence.

" When they compear in court in consequence of their bail he detains them in prison, and when required by instrument to deliver up the prisoners or bail bonds he and his depute refuse both.

" He imposes exorbitant fines on poor people, and hath presently in prison four men fined in a hundred pounds each, and for ought is known not all three are worth a hundred merks Scots, except their poor household furniture, yet they are sentenced to lie in prison till it is paid ; that is for ever."

Whether the protest bore fruit or not we cannot say, but the town house still stands, a silent witness to his enormities.

Opening on the square where the town house stands is also the Auld Kirkyard. It is old, very old, like most of the kirkyards round Scottish Parish Churches, and clustered with grey tombstones set irregularly. Here it is, as mentioned in *When a Man's Single*, that women and children and a few men squeezed through their windows from the Kirk Wynd and dandered pleasantly from grave to grave reading the inscriptions. We should like to say that the

THE WINDOW IN THRUMS

THE AULD LICHT MANSE

NANNY'S COTTAGE

church itself is a handsome structure worthy of its fame, but truth forbids it. To listen to the old Scottish psalm-tunes sung by the noble congregation there is in itself an inspiration.

From the square there also leads off the Kirk Wynd, where Rob Angus, the hero of *When a Man's Single*, had his home. Here also are many relics of old-time Kirriemuir. One of them is the " straight arch " which spans an eight foot opening over Grant's Pend. It is composed of stones which meet together over the lintel, not in an arch, but in a straight line, and is a very interesting relic of old-fashioned masonry. At the other end of the Wynd there is an inscribed lintel, giving the date 1688 and the initials I. F. and B. F., which was the date of the marriage of the couple who inhabited the house. It was an old-fashioned Scottish custom which has long since disappeared. The Wynd itself is as old-fashioned as its name suggests.

The Wynd leads into Bank Street, where once there stood the famous Auld Licht Kirk, which was demolished in 1893. Barrie himself presided at the bazaar held to raise funds for the erection of a new building. This stands at present, a Gothic structure, surmounting some modern shops, a strange combination of utility and beauty. But the Auld Lichts who built it were wise in their generation, for at one stroke they secured their church and the endowment for its upkeep!

The Auld Licht Kirk that Barrie knew is gone for ever. But a photograph of it has happily been preserved, and is reproduced on page 42. There is not much to inspire genius when one looks at it. But Barrie saw it through the warm glow of

Margaret Ogilvy's love for it, and that makes all the difference.

Almost across the way is the doctor's house, conjuring up visions of Dr. McQueen and his little housekeeper Grizel. Where the gig once stood with the pony pawing the cobble-stones, there now splutter the engines of the many chars-à-bancs that make this part of Bank Street the hub of Kirriemuir. Near the doctor's house is a close which no Barrie lover should miss. Go through the close and have a peep at the window above it. There in the house of his old friend, Mr. Mills, Barrie, at the age of seven, saw his first play.

All these things are to be seen around the square, but the visitor to Kirriemuir will be mostly anxious to see the outstanding scenes of Barrie's writings. One of these is the House on the Brae, popularly known as " The Window in Thrums." It is not far off. One just needs to turn southwards from the square, go down a long brae and up another. As he is on his way he is passing through the scene of the battle of the weavers with the military mentioned in *The Little Minister*. At the top of the brae is the house which he is seeking. It stands opposite " Strathview," the house to which Barrie's parents came when they returned to Kirriemuir. The windows of the one house just look right into the other, and it is easy to see, with Barrie living across the road, how easily he found a setting for his story. But we must remember this, if it looks too easy, it is only Barrie who would have found that setting. Dr. Whyte passed by it daily, but he saw nothing of the things that were to be seen in Barrie's books. If it had not been for Barrie, it would be only a little wayside cottage, blinking at the sun.

Living exactly opposite the cottage, Barrie could not fail to describe it well. His description does not fit it to-day, but it fitted exactly forty years ago. "On the bump of green round which the brae twists, at the top of the brae, and within cry of T'nowhead farm, still stands a one-story house, whose whitewashed walls, streaked with the discoloration that rain leaves, look yellow when the snow comes. In the old days the stiff ascent left Thrums behind, and where now is the making of a suburb was only a poor row of dwellings and a manse, with Hendry's cot to watch the brae. The house stood bare without a shrub, in a garden whose paling did not go all the way round, the potato pit being only kept out of the road, that here sets off southward, by a broken dyke of stones and earth. On each side of the slate-coloured door was a window of knotted glass. Ropes were flung over the thatch to keep the roof on in the wind."

Since then the house of the brae has been modernized. A slate roof takes the place of thatch, a garden wall surrounds it, and there are shrubs and flowers in the garden. Some may regret the change, but in private hands it has been inevitable, if it was not to go to rack and ruin.

In all probability he was never inside this little dwelling. The folk he wrote about were not its inmates. Jess, Hendry, and unselfish Leeby, these are his mother, his father, and his sister Jane Ann, all idealized according to his genius. Jamie is a purely literary creation, and perhaps because he is a creature of fancy his character is more illusive than the rest. But they are all real, and

THE LITTLE MINISTER

THE locality Barrie deals with in *The Little Minister* is different from that of *A Window in Thrums*. The setting, of course, is Kirriemuir and district, but he turns away from its southern corner to deal with the north and west. If one could discriminate in his knowledge of Kirriemuir, which is quite impossible, for he knew it as well as he knew his mother's face, one would say that this part is the one he knew best of all. For here he was born and here he lived until his family removed to Forfar.

The first place of interest is his birthplace. It is situated along the Brechin Road, about two hundred yards from the square. The building is known as the Tenements, and the reader of *The Little Minister* will remember his quip about it there. It is overlooked by the Auld Licht Manse. " Every back window in the Tenements has a glint of it, and so the back of the Tenements is always better behaved than the front." It does have the curious feature that the back looks towards the road and the front looks into a yard, which, we are told, was once a cattle yard. It is reached by a broad entrance from the highway, and the visitor in turning through this entrance will stop and look at the house immediately on his left. That is

103

Then follow the names of some of the children and, finally, " David Barrie, died June, 1902, in his 88th year."

The cemetery flanks the Hill of Kirriemuir, which is entered from behind. The reader of *The Little Minister* will remember that here is situated the standing stone where Babbie met Rob Dow's son. He does not at first recognize her as the woman who had been bewitching the Little Minister and driving his father to the drink again. She quizzes him about his troubles. Suddenly he begins to edge away. " You're the woman," he cries from a safe distance. " What makes you think that? " asks Babbie. " Because you're so bonny."

Was ever compliment more delicately paid?

The Toad's Hole where Babbie and the Minister were married is no longer to be found on the Hill. It was filled up many years ago. The writer in searching for it had a rather interesting experience. He came to the place where he thought it might be and discovered a travelling tinker who had just unloosed his pony from the shafts to let it out to grass. " Have you ever heard of a place round here called the Toad's Hole? " he asked at random. " Have I no? " the tinker said. " It was in this very spot years ago afore they filled it up. They used to let us come and stay here afore a' the gentry came. I've seen as many as twenty caravans camped here at one time. But noo we can only bide an hour or twa and let the powny loose." Times are changed since Babbie's day. The Toad's Hole is filled up, the gipsies are gone, and a magnificent cricket pavilion, gifted by Barrie, crowns the site of old romance.

To the north-west of the Hill is Caddam Wood, where so much of the scene of *The Little Minister* is cast. Would that we had the eyes to see it as when " in the moonlight the grass seemed tipped with hoar frost and the shoots of the beeches were like children clustering round their mothers' skirts," and Babbie came singing down the glade, dancing her way into the heart of Gavin. Such visions are not for common men, but the great leafy avenue of Windyghoul still is there, and the cottage where poor old Nanny dwelt. It stands on the edge of the forest, with a slate roof now instead of thatch, but in all essentials just the same. There is the garden and there is the well and there is the light and shade of the forest. Nearby is the Roman road where the legionaries kept vigil against the Picts in the days of long ago.

We must say a word about the well. The one that Barrie wrote of was on the other side of Windyghoul and buried in the wood. It was covered by a huge stone which Bob Angus bore to Caddam, flinging it before him a yard at a time. " The path to it now," says Barrie, " is difficult to find. It is lost in blaeberries and the well itself is choked and dry." We are afraid we must say that there is no such path and there is no such well. A huge stone lies in Caddam Wood, about fifty yards from Nanny's cottage. That is all. A fertile imagination did the rest.

At Nanny's cottage, however, in the garden, there *is* a well; though not the well where Babbie went to draw. It has its glories too, and we would not rob it of them. Did not Sentimental Tommy boast of a well in Thrums, where you drop a pail

THE *SENTIMENTAL TOMMY* BOOKS

BARRIE had now in his successive books practically exhausted the local background supplied by Kirriemuir. *A Window in Thrums* had covered the southern corner. *The Little Minister* had been staged in the west and north. If he was to find a new setting for another story he must rely upon the east. Here there was no romantic manse or even a whitewashed cottage on the brae. But there was the Den, a spacious natural amphitheatre hidden from the highway by a cluster of dingy houses. It was just the very setting for a story of boyhood days. So he took Sentimental Tommy to the Den. And the Painted Lady and Grizel and the sturdy Corp and even Aaron Latta obediently followed after.

"The Den is so craftily hidden away," he says, "that when within a stone's throw you may give up the search for it; it is also so deep that larks rise from the bottom and carol overhead, thinking themselves high in the heavens before they are on a level with Nether Drumley's farmyard. In shape it is almost a semicircle, but its size depends on you and the maid. If she be with you the Den is so large that you must rest here and there; if you are after her boldly, you can dash to the Cuttle Well, which was the trysting-place, in the time a

stout man takes to lace his boots; if you are one
of those self-conscious ones who look behind to see
whether jeering blades are following, you may
crouch and wriggle your way onward and not be
with her in half an hour."

The Den will always be the place where
Sentimental Tommy and his merry men held
high conspiracy. We shall always see them
stealing from the river or clambering down the
crags to meet at the Cuttle Well in the last
Jacobite rising. But we shall not forget those
other dim figures which lurk about its shades.
There are Aaron Latta and his lass sitting beside
the shoaging stone in happy innocence. There
is the Painted Lady and faithful Grizel. And
there are other figures too, dim shades, whose
story was never told, to whom the Cuttle Well
was a place of happy memory. It is only a spring
of water, but all the mysteries of life and love and
death waited upon its music.

It whispers to us of innocence and tragedy and
knowledge that comes too late, all wrapped up in
the bundle of life, never to be disentangled. But
when the glory has faded into grey the chief actors
recall them with a tear or with a smile. "I once
saw an aged woman, a widow of many years, cry
softly at the mention of the Cuttle Well. 'John
was a good man to you,' I said, for John had
been her husband. 'He was a leal man to me,'
she answered with wistful eyes, 'aye, he was a
leal man to me—but it wisna John I was thinking o'. You dinna ken what makes me greet so
sair,' she added presently, and though I thought
I knew now, I was wrong. 'It's because I canna
mind his name,' she said."

THE DEN

THE PINK PATH BY THE BURN

THE SCENE OF THE JACOBITE RISING
(The Reekie Broth Pot is in the background and the Cuttle
Well above the two steps.)

Jean Myles had sat at the Cuttle Well with her sweetheart, Aaron Latta. It was life's rosy morn for them and all the world was young. " Jean Latta," Aaron wrote, capturing the bliss that filled their minds and giving it reality. It was only a mark upon the dust, but it was the pledge and symbol of the happiness to be.

" Jean Sandys," corrected a masterful voice behind them, and their dream was shattered.

It was Magerful Tam, jeering down at them as they lay upon the grass. He had loomed up all unnoticed, a Cyclopean figure from the shades, the ambassador of hell.

" Dinna change the name ! " cried Jean, sensing coming tragedy. " Dinna let him change the name ! "

Aaron wavered and fell. Shuddering at himself, shrinking before this leering devil, ineffectually struggling against a will that was stronger than his own, he changed it. " Jean Sandys " stood written where " Jean Latta " was. And Jean rose up, her womanliness all gone, to go off with Magerful Tam.

She married him, hating him. The women-folk thought she had played Aaron false and they stoned her out of Thrums. " Poor Aaron Latta ! " they said, shocked into pity when they heard his story. No one said, " Poor Jean Myles." She was a bad one. There was none to pity bad ones. Such was the tragedy of the Cuttle Well told in *Sentimental Tommy*.

With artistic economy Barrie brings the son back to the scene of his mother's shame. With all the inconsequence of youth he dances on the grave of his mother's dreams, mumming on the stage of

Aaron Latta's fall. There beside the bubbling of the well can be heard the voices of the Jacobite conspirators, each answering to the call of romance as their parents did before them. Symbolic figures of youth they are, acting their part on the stage of life, blissfully unconscious of the tragedies of age.

To complete the picture of the tragedy that hangs round the Cuttle Well, the Painted Lady comes on the scene, possessed by a devil that might have been an angel. She lives in dreams, only now and then breaking through to the world outside. But when she sees that world it is so horrible she flies back to her dreams again. It is all fantastic and yet so real—woman's weakness—man's selfishness—ignorance and love—no guiding star—till little Grizel comes and brings order into chaos by her unselfish love. He would be dull indeed who could stand beside the Cuttle Well with the recollections of Barrie's book before him and not sense something of the mystery of life.

The Den is a public park now with bandstand and refreshment rooms all complete. A little spoiled it is by their obtrusiveness, but the place is a charming spot. Two mysteries present themselves to him who visits it in quest of Barrie lore. Where was the lair where the conspirators gathered and where was the Painted Lady's house? For neither is in evidence to-day.

The lair, we are quite sure, from the evidence of an old photograph, was behind the Cuttle Well. Barrie himself speaks of it as being on the right side of the burn, and there it undoubtedly was, but it has been filled in and banked up, probably to make room for the pathway that twists above the well. We are glad it is no more, for the memory of the Painted Lady lying there attended by her child is too grisly to be revived in such a happy spot.

The Painted Lady's cottage belongs to the Never Never Land. It existed only in the imagination of the author. The coffin brig which led to it may be found along the road a few yards from the western entrance to the Den, but of the cottage itself not a trace. It will be remembered that the cottage was reached by double dykes that ran at arm's length from each other to help a drunken farmer to negotiate the darkness. There is a place called Doubledykes on the other side of Kirriemuir, and by the side of the two dykes there is a lonely cottar's dwelling, but whether this is the Painted Lady's cottage or no only Barrie himself can say.

THE GLENS

THE GLENS

THE Glens of Clova and Prosen, so well beloved by Barrie, are almost within walking distance of Kirriemuir. We say *almost*, for though they meet at Cortachy, five miles distant from Kirriemuir near the little hamlet of Dykehead, they run for some twelve to fifteen miles into the Grampians. So that the traveller who wishes to see them both had better have some vehicle at his disposal. Let him not be misled by the pedestrian feats of the schoolmaster of Glen Quharity who could go into Thrums and back again from his schoolhouse in the glen in the course of an afternoon. Barrie conveniently reduced the distance for him to a matter of five miles. As a matter of fact the schoolhouse in the glen is seven miles up Glen Clova.

The visitor who starts to walk from Kirriemuir will find a convenient resting-place at Cortachy, which Barrie calls Cullew. There he may enjoy the Highland hospitality of an excellent hotel. At Cortachy also is the old church of which Barrie writes in the *Auld Licht Idylls*. The reader will remember that he refers to a session record there, where there can be read an old minute " announcing that on a certain Sabbath there was no preaching because the minister was away at the burning of a witch." The minute now, unfortunately, has gone, but Barrie's reference was quite correct. Sometime before 1902 it was torn from the minute book by some vandal's hands and has never been recovered. But an extract of it, copied into the minute book of Clova when that church was disjoined from Cortachy in 1860, confirms the author's reference. It states that in 1662 there was no sermon at Cortachy, the minister being at Clova at " the execution of Margaret Adamson, who was burned there for ane witch."

Two other excerpts from the session book of Cortachy are of more than general interest. The first is dated March 22nd, 1674, and states that a delinquent " was this day absolved, having appeared all the former days in sackcloath and stood bearfoot at the church door till publick worship began." This was just after the reformation when the Session and the Presbytery exercised an iron rule over the morals of the parish.

The other minute is of a different tone. It is dated September 18th, 1715, and records that " the minister durst not adventure to goe to Clova, My Lord Drummond and several other rebells being there pressing the people to rise in arms against the Government." It was written, of course, at the time of the first Jacobite rebellion.

Cortachy is the seat of the Airlie family, whose noble Cortachy Castle may be seen surrounded by trees in the valley. Nearby is Tulloch Hill, surmounted by the memorial to the ninth Earl of Airlie, killed in the South African War.

The two glen roads meet at Cortachy, and the one to the right takes the traveller up Glen Clova. This is the Glen Quharity of the Barrie books. The schoolhouse in the glen is a little whitewashed

GLEN CLOVA

THE SCHOOL IN THE GLEN

THE SCHOOLHOUSE IN THE GLEN

building standing by the roadside with the school attached. The school is smaller than the schoolhouse, and the three large diamond-paned windows give it a chapel-like appearance. It is pretty enough in the summer-time, but the picture Barrie gives us of it in the *Auld Licht Idylls* is cold and bleak.

On a summer day, however, with the bees buzzing to the hives in the garden and the flowers flaunting their many-coloured jackets to the sun and the wireless ready to bring one news, in the gloaming it is the embodiment of peace.

The place is known as Wateresk, for the very simple reason that it stands beside the waters of the Esk. Across the river is Waster Lunny's farm, also made famous in *The Little Minister*. Between the schoolhouse and the farm is a suspension bridge, over which the children come on their way to school. The reader will remember Barrie's bridge of chains over which the dominie crawled when he heard of Gavin's death. Perhaps the bridge of chains was there before the suspension bridge. Perhaps Barrie saw the suspension bridge and used his imagination. The reader can have it either way. For our own part, Barrie is at liberty to do anything he likes.

At the head of the glen is the Milton of Clova, containing little more than a church and an hotel. Over the Grampians is Braemar. There is a foot-track from Braemar along which came Queen Victoria in 1861, accompanied by her consort, on a pleasure expedition. But they had the aid of Highland ponies. The traveller had better not attempt the journey on foot unless the weather be exceptionally fine. The crossing is a matter of eighteen miles or so over rough moorland country, and one has to look out for mists. Queen Victoria, we might say, did not complete the journey.

Up Clova way in 1650 there came another royal traveller, but this time on no pleasure expedition. It was Charles II hastening up the glen on his famous " Start " from Perth. He spent one night at Cortachy Castle, then hurried up the glen to break through the Grampians to the north. The good people of the glen were little prepared for his reception, for we are told he spent the night " in a filthy room on an old bolster above a mat of sedges and rushes." He was headed off, however, and forced to return to the Covenanting army, and, incidentally, to those sermons he so much hated.

Glen Prosen, which is reached from Cortachy by skirting Tulloch Hill, has been made known to Barrie readers as the scene of the banishment of Sentimental Tommy. He had to sit an essay competition with a view to entrance to Aberdeen University. The subject of the essay was " A Day in Church " and the writing was to be in Scots. The only other entrant for the scholarship was Lauchlan McLauchlan " who had a flow of words but could no more describe a familiar scene with a pen than a milkmaid can draw a cow." Tommy started well, but in the end of the competition was ignominiously beaten. He had stuck for a word in Scots to describe a half-filled church, and could not go on till he had found it. *Manzy, mask, flow, curran, middling full, fell mask*, these were all candidates for his choice, only to be rejected. *Hantle* was the word he found—too late.

To qualify him for something other than the

literary life, Aaron Latta sent him to the Dubb of Prosen, where there was a vacancy at the herding.

The scenery of Prosen is not so grand as that of Clova, but it has a rustic beauty of its own. Deer forests sweep down to the road, and the traveller may often see the gentle animals coming down to drink. As one emerges from the forests, the road winds round the northern hillside of the glen, and a long vista of peaceful pasture-land stretches for miles before the view. It is not rugged beauty like Glen Clova, where the towering Grampians never relax their frowning face. It is rather the quiet beauty of a sheltered valley which makes one say, " Here I would like to come when I am tired, and rest." And here, responding to that call, there did come in bygone days two striving men who desired sweet calm to prepare for a great adventure from which, alas, they did not return.

On the roadside in Prosen, just where the road debouches on the hill, there stands a memorial to Captain Scott and Edward Wilson, who spent a holiday here before their last Antarctic journey. Knowing Scott's friendship with Barrie we need hardly surmise who it was who sent him to this quiet northern glen. The memorial is a fountain erected by the surrounding folk who had grown to love both him and his companion. It bears the following inscription, " Given to the care of the people of Cortachy for them to hold in remembrance of Robert Falcon Scott and Edward Adrian Wilson, who knew this glen. They reached the South Pole on 17th January, 1912, and died together on the great ice barrier, March, 1912.

HERE AND THERE THROUGH ANGUS

IN none of his books does Barrie give us any adequate conception of the beauty of his county. His interest does not lie in nature, and when he tries his hand at description he soon tires. He seems, moreover, to realize his own weakness in this respect and to leave description alone. " Never will I describe my glen," he says through the mouth of the schoolmaster in *The Little Minister*, and this is typical of his attitude as a whole.

There are perhaps one or two reasons for this. In the first place, Barrie had a journalistic training, and the journalist knows that the folk who read the newspaper in the morning are not so much interested in nature as in human nature. It is the foibles and loves and general doings of his fellows that the average man is interested in, and it is because Barrie deals so exclusively with these that he attains so wide an appeal.

Again, he left Kirriemuir and its district when he was very young and spent most of his life in the city. To city life he seems to be drawn by an irresistible inclination. He is never far away from London. Therefore when he wrote of the men and women he had known he treated them merely as human beings in another environment than his own—an environment that was quaint and old-fashioned, but which owed little to the waving of the corn and the grandeur of the hills.

Moreover, he wrote his Thrums books for the most part when away from Kirriemuir. He could not, therefore, see things in delicate detail. His sketches of nature are just broad impressions which had lodged themselves in his memory. But we must not imagine from his neglect of the beauty of his birthplace that it is devoid of natural charm. The town itself has little to show in the way of architecture, but it is quaint and old-fashioned with its crooked streets and narrow closes and its low-roofed, heavily slated houses. One afternoon in it, however, exhausts its possibilities, architecturally or otherwise.

It is different with the surrounding country. That is magnificent. Five hundred yards away from the centre of the town there stands the Hill. We have already described the view as seen from the cemetery. On the Hill the country round about appears even more magnificent. One sees a vista of fertile valley, studded with whitewashed farmsteads, and sombre woods, and green fields stretching as far as Stirling on the west, and sweeping almost to the seashore on the east. The Sidlaws break the southern contour, with Forfar and its glistening loch lying in the hollow. Behind one the Grampians tower peak on peak, with the monument of Airlie keeping sentinel at the entrance to the glens.

The nearest glens of Prosen and Clova, which are only five miles distant, provide mountain scenery of the grandest order. A drive to the head of Clova is good for both body and soul. It is grand, but not too grand. The hills do not

FORFAR—FROM BALMASHANNER HILL.
(The Tilliedrum of Barrie's novels)

oppress one with a sense of ruthlessness. The cry of the curlew may be wild in the ear, but the whirring of the reaper in the valley adds a touch of domesticity to the scene. The place is friendly.

Prosen is more wooded and the hills more gentle. It has not the rugged masculinity of Clova. It lies more to the south and smiles at one in the sun. It suggests picnics, and camp-fires in the gloaming, and rest.

All around there are other glens we have not mentioned, as they fail to come into the Barrie story. But there is fair Glen Isla, with the Bonnie Hoose o' Airlie in its midst trying to pierce the Grampians to the west. There is charming little Glen Ogil in the east, with the long expanse of the Forfar waterworks. There is dark Glen Shee, stretching for miles in rugged grandeur. Kirriemuir is the gateway to all of them.

When we turn southwards from the little town into the valley of Strathmore, other delights and recompenses meet the eye. No river other than the humble Dean flows through the Strath, but the missing place is taken by a series of extensive lochs. There is the Loch of Forfar, owned by Earl of Strathmore, free to any person who desires to walk around it. Here, in the olden days, Queen Margaret had her residence, when Malcolm Canmore occupied the castle in the town. Farther east there is Rescobie Loch, sacred to the memory of St. Triduana, who is said to have dwelt by its shore and worked healing among the blind when the monks first came to Scotland. Eastwards still is Balgavies Loch, nine miles from the sea.

The scene from the top of the Hill of Kirriemuir

is repeated from the Hill of Balmashanner, which stands behind Forfar to the south. There, from the top of its War Memorial, the lovely vale of Strathmore spreads itself before us, while the old grey town of Forfar lies sleeping at our feet. A rest-house offers shelter from the wind and leisure to view the beauties of the scene. On the top of the War Memorial is a mountain indicator, whence all the peaks of the Grampians in view may easily be identified.

Forfar itself is a quiet town, with cobbled streets and wynds and closes for him who has an eye for that kind of thing. The old town hall in the square boasts pictures by Raeburn and Romney. A mile to the east of the town stands Restenneth Priory, mentioned in the first chapter of this book. Near by it runs the old Roman road from Battledykes to Kirkbuddo.

In the valley of Strathmore in which Forfar lies there are many stately castles and old-world mansions. Angus is rich in these histories in stone, for, being entirely agricultural, it has hardly been touched by the rush of modern progress. Chief among them all is the noble pile of Glamis. It dates from the fifteenth century in its older portions, and if its walls could speak they could tell us many a story. In 1562 the ill-starred Mary Queen of Scots flew her banner on its tower as she rested there for the night on her way to the Northern counties to suppress the rebellion of Huntly. Again, in 1716, it welcomed the Chevalier de St. George in his attempt to rouse the Highlanders to win back his father's crown. In 1793 it saw Sir Walter Scott.

Scott was well acquainted with the Angus

country. Arbroath, the " Redlintie " of *Senti-mental Tommy*, is the " Fairport " of *The Antiquary*. The people of these two novels are separated by a period of only fifty years, so that Barrie's sons and daughters are Scott's grand-children. Barrie has lately said that he would like to meet Sir Walter. Perhaps Sir Walter would like to meet Sir James. Have they something to say to each other about the Angus folk? Will Sir Walter suggest to Sir James that the humour and pathos of his characters are slightly over-drawn? Will Sir James suggest to Sir Walter that he was only a stranger amongst them and never knew them? If they arrange debates in Elysium, we must endeavour to be there.

INDEX

INDEX

INDEX